Spot the Differences
Hedgehog or Porcupine?

by Jamie Rice

Bullfrog Books

Ideas for Parents and Teachers

Bullfrog Books let children practice reading informational text at the earliest reading levels. Repetition, familiar words, and photo labels support early readers.

Before Reading

- Discuss the cover photo. What does it tell them?

- Look at the picture glossary together. Read and discuss the words.

Read the Book

- "Walk" through the book and look at the photos. Let the child ask questions. Point out the photo labels.

- Read the book to the child, or have him or her read independently.

After Reading

- Prompt the child to think more. Ask: What did you know about hedgehogs and porcupines before reading this book? What more would you like to learn?

Bullfrog Books are published by Jump!
5357 Penn Avenue South
Minneapolis, MN 55419
www.jumplibrary.com

Library of Congress Cataloging-in-Publication Data

Names: Rice, Jamie, author.
Title: Hedgehog or porcupine? / by Jamie Rice.
Description: Minneapolis, MN: Jump!, Inc., [2023]
Series: Spot the differences | Includes index.
Audience: Ages 5–8
Identifiers: LCCN 2022011711 (print)
LCCN 2022011712 (ebook)
ISBN 9798885241670 (hardcover)
ISBN 9798885241687 (paperback)
ISBN 9798885241694 (ebook)
Subjects: LCSH: Hedgehogs—Juvenile literature.
Porcupines—Juvenile literature.
Classification: LCC QL737.E753 R53 2023 (print)
LCC QL737.E753 (ebook) | DDC 599.33/2—dc23/eng/20220407
LC record available at https://lccn.loc.gov/2022011711
LC ebook record available at https://lccn.loc.gov/2022011712

Editor: Katie Chanez
Designer: Emma Bersie

Photo Credits: Eric Isselee/Shutterstock, cover (left), 1 (left), 21, 24 (top); Csanad Kiss/Shutterstock, cover (right); KAMONRAT/Shutterstock, 1 (right); Coatsey/Alamy, 3, 10–11, 23br; Proshkin Aleksandr/Shutterstock, 4; Amelia Martin/Shutterstock, 5; Kzenon/Shutterstock, 6–7 (top); Holly Kuchera/Shutterstock, 6–7 (bottom), 23bl; vanchai/Shutterstock, 8–9, 23tr; John E Marriott/All Canada Photos/SuperStock, 12–13; Dan Sullivan/Alamy, 14–15; Rita Petcu/Shutterstock, 15, 23tl; Coatesy/Shutterstock, 16–17, 22 (left); Brian Bevananthe/Mary Evans Picture Library/SuperStock, 18–19; irin-k/Shutterstock, 20; Gerald Corsi/iStock, 22 (right); Nynke van Holten/Shutterstock, 24 (bottom).

Printed in the United States of America at Corporate Graphics in North Mankato, Minnesota.

Table of Contents

How do they stay safe?
A hedgehog rolls into a ball.
A porcupine points its quills.
Which is this?

How to Use This Book

In this book, you will see pictures of both hedgehogs and porcupines. Can you tell which one is in each picture?

Hint: You can find the answers if you flip the book upside down!

Look Out for Quills!

This is a hedgehog.

This is a porcupine.

They look alike.

But they have differences.

Can you spot them?

Let's see!

Look out!

Both have sharp quills.

A hedgehog's are short.

A porcupine's are long.

Whose quills are these?

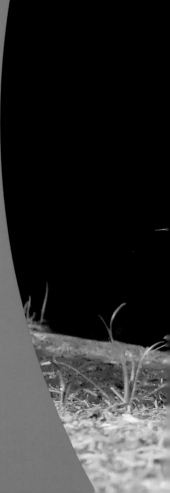

Answer: porcupine

quill

How do they stay safe?

A hedgehog rolls into a ball.

A porcupine points its quills.

Which is this?

A hedgehog's tail is short.

It is hard to see.

A porcupine's is long.

Which is this?

Answer: porcupine

tail

A hedgehog has small feet and short claws.

A porcupine has big feet and long claws.

Which is this?

claw

A hedgehog's nose
is pointed.

A porcupine's is flat.

Which is this?

Answer: hedgehog

worm

A hedgehog eats bugs.
A porcupine eats leaves.
Yum!
Who eats this snack?

See and Compare

short quills

short tail

pointed nose

small feet

short claws

Porcupine

long quills

flat nose

long tail

big feet

long claws

Quick Facts

Hedgehogs and porcupines have quills. Quills protect them from predators. They live in many habitats, including forests and grasslands. They are similar, but they have differences. Take a look!

Hedgehogs

- have around 5,000 quills
- build nests on the ground under plants and leaves
- hibernate in winter
- mainly eat insects

Porcupines

- have around 30,000 quills
- build nests or dens between rocks or inside hollow trees
- do not hibernate in winter
- only eat plants

Picture Glossary

claws
Hard, sharp nails on the feet of some animals.

points
Aims at something.

quills
Hollow, hard, sharp growths on the bodies of some animals.

sharp
Having an edge or point that cuts or pierces easily.

Index

To Learn More

Finding more information is as easy as 1, 2, 3.

❶ Go to www.factsurfer.com

❷ Enter "hedgehogorporcupine?" into the search box.

❸ Choose your book to see a list of websites.